W9-AXY-814

WITHDRAWN

A GIFT
from CHILDHOOD

MEMORIES OF AN AFRICAN BOYHOOD

BABA WAGUÉ DIAKITÉ

GROUNDWOOD BOOKS | HOUSE *of* ANANSI PRESS
TORONTO   BERKELEY

Groundwood Books / House of Anansi Press
110 Spadina Avenue, Suite 801, Toronto, Ontario M5V 2K4
or c/o Publishers Group West
1700 Fourth Street, Berkeley, CA 94710

We acknowledge for their financial support of our publishing program the Government of Canada through the Book Publishing Industry Development Program (BPIDP).

Library and Archives Canada Cataloguing in Publication

Diakité, Baba Wagué
A gift from childhood : memories of an African boyhood / Baba Wagué Diakité.

ISBN 978-0-88899-931-3

1. Diakité, Baba Wagué–Childhood and youth. 2. Mali–Biography–Juvenile literature. 3. Mali–Social life and customs–Juvenile literature. I. Title.

PS3554 I222Z43 2010   j813'.54   C2009-904753-5

Design by Michael Solomon
The illustrations are on earthenware tiles, painted with underglaze colors and fired.
Printed and bound in China

Den be i ko bogo kènè. A mana dilan cogo min,
a bè ja o cogo la.

"A child is simply like wet clay.
It dries with the shape it is given."

This book is dedicated to the elders
of Kassaro who helped shape me.

A special thank-you to
Gloria Neuenschwander.

A LITTLE BOY sat on the dirt floor with a bowl of millet porridge between his legs. He screamed at the top of his lungs.

"*Nay t'a fay! Nay t'aka sari fay!* I don't like it! I don't like your porridge! It has no sugar. It has no milk."

"Eat it, Baba Wagué," Grandma Sabou said gently. "It is good for you."

The boy kicked his legs wildly. "*Nay bay taa n'fa fey.* I want to go back to *n'fa* — my father! He has everything!"

This was the beginning of Baba's new life in the village. Before this, he had lived with his parents in the city, with its rich variety of food.

Every time Baba behaved in this manner, Grandma Sabou would calmly get up and go to rest on her bamboo bed, letting the boy cry until he was exhausted. Then Baba's forehead would slowly drift onto his right knee, and he would sleep for a good hour.

When he awoke, he would be hungry enough to eat the entire bowl of sticky porridge.

Grandma would smile and say, "The best time to do something is when you are willing to do it. Baba, you did a good job."

This was the daily routine between Baba and his grandmother. It was difficult, but Grandma and Baba managed to find the best sides of each other. Eventually, Baba adapted to village life, and soon he happily helped Grandma do small chores around the compound.

✳

I was only four rainy seasons old when I first came to the village. My parents decided to send me and my two older brothers there to be raised by our paternal grandparents. This was the way it had been done in the family for many generations.

But my grandparents, who had sixteen children of their own, did not have that privilege and help. Their children were born during the time of the French occupation of West Africa. It was a confusing time, interfering with family structures and, in some cases, forcing families apart. More than a century of European occupation greatly contributed to the loss of cultures and traditions for one whole generation of Africans.

The greatest damage was losing the crucial links to the ancestral way of life. Today, Africans are left with an irretrievable gap between themselves and their pre-colonial ancestors.

I was lucky to be given the gift of storytelling by my elders. It was their wish that I not only learn from these stories, but that I pass them on to the next generation and the generation after that.

I feel privileged to explain to others the history and

value of storytelling, and how it has been used as a tool for teaching, not just for entertaining. This important source of knowledge is slowly vanishing from many of our cultures. With the stories I have heard from my elders, I have come to understand a little of the way our pre-colonial ancestors lived — respecting others and living in harmony with nature.

The oral historians in Mali have often said, "No matter how cloudy the past may look, the bright future will be born from it."

If you know where you came from, you will know where you are heading.

Kassaro

My parents wanted my brothers and me to know where we came from and to have the opportunity to meet our larger family — something they never had the chance to do when they were growing up. At the time, I did not clearly see why I was sent to my father's native town for many years. But life in the village of Kassaro turned out to be a great experience.

During this time, there were fewer than five thousand people in the community. Like everyone else, my family did both farming and ranching. We had acres of land that surrounded our home compound. The compound itself was a big courtyard ringed with round and square adobe houses facing inward. It housed our family in a circle of life with fathers, mothers, uncles, aunts, grandparents, cousins, brothers and sisters.

It was a great place for children to grow up and learn the importance of respect, especially for the elders who preceded us on earth. However, no one was left out, since everyone had to respect the person who was even a year older. Children learned and practiced this respect by

touring the compound every morning and evening, going door-to-door greeting their elders. At the same time, the youngest were watched over and cared for by all of their elders.

The central part of the compound was the arena for daily activities such as cooking, washing clothes, braiding hair and bathing children. It was also the gathering place for storytelling, meetings, solving problems and entertaining guests. Everyone was required to be present at mealtimes. If you missed a meal, no special treatment was arranged.

Splitting into groups, we gathered around the big community bowls in the courtyard to share the meal of the day. Children were always encouraged to show respect for the meal by not chatting while they ate, showing their appreciation for the grains that nourish us. Sometimes it was so crowded that we had to sit shoulder-to-shoulder in concentric circles — adults behind children. This was the goal: bringing everyone together to feel closeness, acceptance, harmony and tolerance. With these values there was the hope and expectation that the youngsters would grow up with good character. The outside world would notice and see that the children from the Diakité family were well brought up.

"One must first look good inside before looking good outside," the elders would tell us.

Our block-long compound was situated in the middle of a large area of farmland called so-foro, the home farm. This entire area was surrounded by beautiful tall acacias, cacti, bamboo and palm trees. Small baobab, wild fig, shea, bumbun and nere trees, mugubagani bushes and many different species of mango were scattered on the farm. All were native to the land except for the mango trees, which had been planted by relatives who helped to clear the land. Each mango tree was named after the person who had planted it.

In addition to those shady mango trees, Grandma Sabou had planted many other small trees and plants. She was an herbalist who had great knowledge of the fruits, leaves, barks, seeds and roots that were remedies for different illnesses. For example, lime and lemon trees could be used to make a good warm tea for colds and for cleansing the body. Guava leaves were helpful for diabetes. Papaya and basil were good for stomach problems and malaria, and the new sprouts from the mango trees could help treat a cough. Shea butter was used for coughs and chest congestion. She knew the healing qualities of many other small plants unknown in other regions.

Grandpa Samba did not know much about herbal healing, but he was a great cook and gardener. He loved nature. He had his own mango plantation called Mangoroforo, about a mile northeast of the compound near a swamp where weaver birds, parrots and other birds made their home. The plantation did not lack for water, so his mango trees grew tall and green above the land.

Samba also cultivated a small field of peanuts around the grove of mangoes. This way he could spend more time watching the birds, whom he considered to be his friends. He spent an abundance of his time watching his bird friends feeding from the wild berry trees.

People would often say, "Samba, you'd better watch over those mangoes closely before the wildlife devours them all."

Grandpa Samba would respond, "I will do what I can, but we all have to eat somehow."

But when the mangoes and groundnuts were ready for

picking, the area became a serious attraction for wildlife and, as predicted, the fields were half eaten by birds, bats, bush rats and squirrels.

In the end Grandma Sabou had enough of this game.

"Your stubbornness will never pay off for what is best for all of your family!" she would shout angrily.

But Grandpa Samba responded delicately as he always did, "I've taken in all that you have said, Sabou. But all of us living creatures must eat somewhere!"

Grandpa Samba

EVEN THOUGH Samba was considered a stubborn man by some, he was also appreciated for his determination. After all, it was his hardheadedness and outspoken manner that had earned him recognition in the early 1900s in his grandfather's village.

This is what Uncle Seku, one of Samba's many sons, told me:

＊

YOUR GRANDPA *Samba was born in the late 1800s, when his father Jaturu was the chief. Samba was the oldest of several children. As a young man, he gained much wisdom from his father, who kept him close in the dugutigui blon — the chief's council chamber where the town problems were solved. Samba watched and learned diplomacy from his elders, and with all these experiences he came to Bomboti, his grandfather Soriba's town.*

He took care of his grandfather, becoming his moving feet and seeing eyes. Since the old man was often caught up with old-age problems, young Samba would sometimes fill in for his grandfather in the town affairs, helping to watch over the village. Because of his respectful nature and his bright vision, the other elders accepted Samba. This is how he earned great respect and became Bomboti's new favorite young advisor.

People praised Soriba.

"The entire body of a child is gold except his head," they said, "and it takes a dedicated elder to transform that head into gold. You, Soriba, have done well with your children, and your grandchildren are following that path. We are glad Samba is here in Bomboti to show other inexperienced youngsters what is meant when elders say, 'When the child learns to wash his hands properly, he will dine with his elders.'"

Late one morning, the people of Bomboti were shaken by the sudden appearance of some unusual visitors. A small handful of French colonialists, guided by their general, were seen advancing toward the town square where Samba and many young men were resting in the shade of a large nere tree.

The nervous villagers, who had heard of but had never seen Europeans before, ran off and hid in their straw huts.

Samba suddenly found himself standing all alone in the wide open square, waiting for the unfamiliar faces to come up to him.

"I do not speak French," he said to himself, "but greetings cannot be mistaken even by a fool."

He stood straight, tall and sure, intending to defend his grandfather's town from these predators at any cost.

Samba knew that he did not need to speak French to understand the intention of the newcomers. As one Malian proverb says, "One need not be where wild animals drink water to know that they don't drink from a gourd."

So Samba suspected that the presence of the general and his men meant only one of two things — they had come to collect taxes from his people or recruit men for their army.

Bravely standing face-to-face with the unexpected visitors, Samba motioned to the intruders that they must go no farther, and the townspeople were inspired to come out and support him.

But the general and his men continued to walk into town.

Samba stood his ground with the townspeople and threw his hands up in the air to tell them to stop. He was slapped on the face and roughly thrown to the ground by the general.

Shocked and outraged, Samba instantly got to his feet and raised his hand against the general. His fellow villagers feared what would become of him.

Before he was able to slap the general back, he was quickly grabbed by two of the general's men, who walked him away to their camp.

The village people were upset and worried. They waited for days, but there was no news of Samba.

After three days, his grandfather Soriba had had enough. Despite the fact that his strength was weakened by old age, he managed with the help of his walking cane and much determination to make it to the camp, where he demanded the return of his grandson.

Later that day, everyone was surprised to see Samba and Soriba return unharmed.

They cheered loudly, "It is he who does not recognize a lion cub who will pick it up by its tail."

Now Samba's fame spread far and wide. In honor of standing up for his people, he was given the nickname Banfulakoro Samba — the Samba who refused to be driven away from his homeland.

Indeed, even the general and his men found his

courage and outspoken manner useful. After trying many twisted, windy and intricate patterns of communication, they finally found ways to communicate with each other after a good meal.

As the Malian people say, "A hidden illness is hard to cure."

From that time on, Samba was invited back several times to the French camp instead of being taken against his will. At times he became the advocate for his people and facilitated arbitration between the Europeans and other villages. Slowly his French improved, and his friendship with the general developed beyond expectation.

Finally Samba, his grandfather Soriba and the townspeople invited their new friends to enter Bomboti. This time the general and his men were welcomed with proper ceremony and food.

Soriba delivered a short but meaningful message to all: "Fortunately, brains do not have any bone. That is what allowed us people to be flexible. One can always change his mind in any direction he desires. So help me to welcome our new friends."

✳

WHEN THE TIME came for the French to move on to explore other parts of West Africa, the general and his men did not forget Soriba's message of reasonableness and flexibility. They often surprised the people of Bomboti by coming to see Soriba and Samba, and they became friends of the family. Because of their good relationship, Samba was invited to visit many places in French West Africa. He was honored by General Gouraud with a medal for his assistance in promoting peaceful relations with the French.

Even after the independence of Mali in the 1960s, French friends continued to visit Banfulakoro Samba and his family every now and then. He learned French cooking, which he often demonstrated with pride to his wife, Sabou. He even inspired two of his own sons to become professional cooks, while many of his other boys joined the Military Committee for National Liberation.

He was often criticized for cooking, giving up his rightful man spot and messing with women's duties.

Grandpa Samba responded, "You have no idea why many women like cooking. It's a form of art, and a very tasty one."

But of all the great things Grandpa Samba did, he considered meeting and marrying Sabou Diakité the most important. Grandpa Samba and Grandma Sabou lived a good life and had sixty long years of marriage. They had many children and worked hard managing and growing food on the many acres of land they were awarded by the Jamanatigui — the head of the people in the region.

At the ceremony, the Jamanatigui presented the land to them with this statement: "There are two things in this world that are given to us by our Maker. First is water and second is earth. They are the ingredients of each individual body. I feel a fool to give something that is already a part of you. But it is for that same reason that you should have this land. Take care of it."

In those days, a man's words were his signature, not

only to the rest of the world but, most importantly, to his own family. If one's words did not align with one's conduct, this could reflect on the entire family for generations.

So, upon accepting the land, it was important for my grandparents to consider all of the wildlife that had been already living there.

Lizards were among the first creatures on the land, even before Grandma Sabou and Grandpa Samba came to clear it. Thus, after the compound was built, the lizards still roamed freely, going anywhere they wanted. Often hungry lizards would steal food from children's bowls. Kids would have loved to catch them and eat them, but the elders were very protective of these sneaky creatures. They thought of them as old spirits of the land. They were also very helpful, eating mosquitoes and other insects.

The elders also spared the lives of a few landmark trees, including one very important wild fig tree called Torow-Sumba — Mother Fig Tree. Fig trees are considered to be magical, as they bear fruit from no blossom. The blossoms are considered invisible to man. They are also long-lived, connecting new generations to their ancestors.

Torow-Sumba remains one of the few trees that were not planted by someone in the family. As years passed, it grew large and high above the landscape. People visited from far and near to pay respect to this massive tree, recognized as the oldest and largest fig tree in the region.

But to my family, this tree is more than an historic landmark. It is a part of the family history and represents the spirits of our ancestors, since many generations have been buried beneath its branches.

This remarkable old tree always bore divine-tasting fruit, creating a feeding place and a home for parrots and other colorful birds that chanted sweet songs all day long from its branches. Grandma said that these songs were meaningful messages that only people with special talents could interpret. The songs sometimes forecast events such as storms, or good and bad fortunes.

Grandpa Samba was not an elegant storyteller like Grandma, but he liked birds and often whistled along with them. He urged his grandchildren to pay attention to the birds' beautiful sounds and listen to their messages.

"Birds are like angels. They feel and predict things through their songs that are hidden from human minds and feelings," he told us. "If one can gather the sounds of all the birds into harmony, that person will find the secret of creation."

Grandpa would use this story to send children off to the old fig tree, telling them to listen to the sweet sounds of the birds and to try to interpret them.

"This can make you very, very smart," he told us.

But, of course, as soon as we children were out of sight, Grandpa would position himself comfortably in his hammock and begin snoring away. When we returned from the field with our minds loaded with questions, Grandpa would be energized by his nap to talk more about the birds and their messages.

The old fig tree continues to be recognized as a true treasure, still attracting birds and visitors from nearby towns. The family now celebrates its existence at the end of each rainy season.

Catching Catfish

JUST AT THE eastern edge of the compound property, Grandma Sabou had her rice field. I had often accompanied her to her field, collecting small pebbles along the way to fill my pockets. While Grandma pulled weeds, I tossed my stones into the bamboo forest to scare small birds away from the rice.

One very special day, Grandma Sabou took me into the middle of the swamp near her muddy rice field to instruct me how to catch a slippery catfish.

As I watched carefully, she detected a slow-moving catfish and tried to pin it down in the muddy blue-gray water. She wrestled with it for quite some time, splashing dark mud in the air, covering her head and face.

It was a very challenging moment, but Grandma Sabou was strong, and she clung tightly to that stubborn, slippery fish.

I wanted to assist Grandma, but the flying mud prevented me from going too close. The mud wrestling came to a sudden stop at the edge of the muddy pool as Grandma emerged between tall grass stalks, exhausted and breath-less.

She crawled out on her elbows and knees toward the bank like a salamander. For an instant she looked like a ghost. Only her two eyes were free of mud.

I stood on the shore, raising my hands and cheering.

"*Ekolo ka kaynay!* You are so strong, Grandma!"

Lying on her chest near the bank, Grandma peered at me, and we both burst into wild laughter. With all her might she threw the catfish onto the dry land. Then she stood up on her strong legs, while the dark gray river mud dripped from her body like rain.

"We learn something new every time we do it! Don't we?" Grandma gasped, catching her breath and smiling.

I nodded.

"Now it is your turn to try, Baba," she said.

I froze, thinking about wrestling a catfish.

"Grandma," I said, "these catfish are very big."

But Grandma responded, "Come on, Baba. Let's have fun!"

Carefully, the two of us walked through the tall grass stalks to the middle of the muddy field.

"If the movement is fast and continuous, it could be a river rat. They taste good, too, but it's really hard to catch them," she whispered. "But if the movement is slow and steady, then it is a catfish." We stood motionless, watching for any telltale signs.

At the first quivering of the grass stalks, we threw stones in that area. Sure enough, there emerged a large catfish with its long moustache. Grandma then instructed me

how to grab the fish by its head and tail, the least slippery areas.

I prepared for the battle by removing my shirt, exposing my bony, skinny body to the bright sunlight.

"Are you going to be standing right here?" I asked.

Grandma nodded and smiled.

I bent over the thick grass stalks and spread my legs apart for strength. Slowly lowering my hands into the muddy water, I lunged for the head and tail of the catfish.

Splashing wildly, that fish mysteriously disappeared somewhere in the muddy field.

Soon we spotted another smaller fish near the same area. This time I aimed before I plunged on my belly to grab the slippery catfish. The wrestling began instantly as I quickly discovered the strength of a single fish in the water.

"Grab it by its head and tail, Baba," shouted Grandma.

The wrestling went on a bit longer than we had anticipated. When I finally got a good grip on the ends of that fish, I began walking with wobbly steps toward the shore. I raised my catch above my head with pride.

"*A filé, Mama,*" I shouted. "Here it is, Grandma."

Then I tossed it onto the dry land far away, so it would not be able to swim back to the water, and Grandma threw a dry cloth over the fish to blindfold it.

By this time the catfish was already covered with dry dirt. I brushed its long body clean and grabbed hold of it firmly as I raised it up to the sky once more.

Grandma began to sing.

"One hero cannot solve all the world's problems.
Every hero comes at his own time.
And here is one looming up right now."

From that moment, I enjoyed my new game, and eventually I introduced other boys in town to the techniques of catching catfish. With the fish I would bring home each time, Grandma would make delicious catfish soup for everyone to enjoy.

"Spicy catfish is good for colds and joints," said Grandma Sabou.

Grandma Sabou the Herbalist

SOMETIMES, even before supper was over, the compound would be crowded with mothers carrying their sick children in their arms, waiting patiently for Grandma's treatment and words of advice.

But I clearly came to understand why Grandma was needed so much when I was stricken with malaria.

My eyes turned yellow and I vomited everything I ate. I shook violently from fever.

Grandma rushed to the outskirts of town and collected leaves from the bitter kinkeliba bush to make some hot tea with honey, lime and fresh basil leaf. After three days of this treatment three times a day, my high fever slowly drifted away. I began to feel better, and after one week, I was myself again.

Afterward, I remembered the sweet aroma and the delicious taste of that hot tea, and I asked Grandma if she would teach me how to make it.

She started her instruction by describing all the telltale signs of malaria. The tea was the easy part that followed.

That simple tea recipe was the beginning of learning

Grandma's secrets of herbal medicines. In a few months I could identify several different herbs, bushes and trees and their uses in traditional healing. Soon villagers who saw me here and there digging roots or clipping leaves for Grandma began calling me Grandma's Herbal Boy.

All of these experiences only strengthened the bond between Grandma and me, and we became inseparable. We often walked home from the fields holding hands and sharing little stories about nature and plants' mysterious ways of healing. We found many of these native plants and bushes short distances from town — kinkeliba for malaria, batti-lili for stomach aches, shea butter for the common cold.

Grandma Sabou helped many sick people in the region, both adults and children. But the queen of healing could not cure everyone. In the case of Garantigui, her own granddaughter, she tried everything she knew, but nothing was able to help the little girl with the swollen belly.

Garantigui was only five rainy seasons old, and she had been under Grandma's care for almost a year. One day, her illness was at its worst. The child had a high fever through the night and into the next day. She hummed from the pain in her stomach.

Grandma checked her eyes and immediately rushed to the outskirts of town to collect some special herbs that only she could identify for Garantigui's blown-up belly. There weren't any other adults around the compound that day to help her. They were all still out farming.

Grandma had no choice but to trust me to watch over my sick little cousin, who was lying on her woven straw

mat covered with her favorite multi-colored blanket. She looked beautiful and peaceful with her gorgeous large eyes.

Garantigui often gazed at me as I sat next to her on a little wooden stool. She began to make her humming noises as she always did when she needed something.

"What do you need?" I asked. "Do you want water?"

After a drink from a small gourd, Garantigui raised her

two arms in the air despite being so weak. I gently bent over and scooped her up onto my lap and looked closely into her perfectly round face, then massaged her head gently to comfort her.

Garantigui responded with a beautiful smile. Then she closed her eyes to take her usual short nap.

I crawled on my knees to place her back on her straw mat, but she suddenly began to tremble, and so I quickly scooped her up again and called her name.

"Garantigui!"

Three times I called her name, but she did not respond. I began to worry as I stared at the empty walls of the room, hoping that Grandma would return soon.

When Grandma Sabou returned from the bush, her hands were filled with colorful red, green and brown leaves. She hurried toward a ceramic pot to boil the herbs for the little girl. Then she peeked into her room.

She leaned against the doorway, staring silently at Garantigui and me. I was only ten rainy seasons old and knew little or nothing of what was going on.

Suddenly the room felt quiet and cold. Garantigui's muscles no longer flexed. She lay peacefully in my arms.

Before Grandma said a word, big tears began to roll down her cheeks, and that was when I understood.

Life had faded out of Garantigui's tiny body.

I was so shocked that I was unable to cry. I kept swallowing my saliva to prevent crying sounds from coming out of my mouth.

Friends and neighbors gathered in the compound for Garantigui's burial ceremony. She was covered with her

favorite blanket and was buried under the big old fig tree beside the other family graves.

Grandma Sabou sang a little song to close the ceremony. The song was about love, strength and courage.

For both Grandma and myself, Garantigui's death was not just a test of strength in life but also a personal matter, as we were so close to her that final year.

Many other children died in the village that year due to malaria, hunger and malnutrition from the big ten-year drought that beat at West Africa through the 1970s. In its path, many new illnesses in the region sprouted up and rained down like insects.

The effect of this drought clouded people's minds for a long while. As much as they tried to settle back to the normal routine of life, it was not easy, as everyone in town had lost a loved one, a friend, or an entire herd of animals.

I was lucky to be among those children who had been vaccinated earlier that year. However, I was still not totally immune from some small sicknesses that brushed me every now and then.

Before I could lay Garantigui's death to rest, I asked Grandma, "What happens to people when they die?"

Grandma clasped her hands together as she always did when she had something important to say.

"See those?" She pointed at a fast-drifting gray cloud, the shade from a shea butter tree and a long-necked bird sitting on a fence. "Those are our ancestors' spirits."

"So what do you think our family spirit will be, Grandma?" I asked.

"I don't know. It could be shade for others to rest under,

a bird to warn them about events, or even a rain cloud to give them hope."

I nodded. I began to understand why she always protested the killing of small creatures around the compound, as they could very well be our ancestors.

Grandma the Storyteller

EVENTUALLY the drought lifted, and our family returned to their usual activities. Grandma also continued to share her wisdom through stories. But this time the stories were not only about animals. She also began to tell tales about people. Some transformed into mountains, some into trees, and others transformed into creatures.

One evening she shared this memorable story about an unusual character who routinely visited the town of Sumamburu.

✳

THERE WAS ONCE *a happy farming town named Sumamburu. The people were compassionate and welcoming. But they had a visitor who came to town every now and then. He was a fine-looking gentleman with a great sense of humor. People liked him, but they were also suspicious of his presence in their town, as misfortune seemed to follow each of his visits.*

Grandma told this story as if we the listeners were present in the town. Her voice expressed sadness or happiness as if she were there also.

After a few years, the people of Sumamburu came to understand that this fine gentleman with a good sense of humor was indeed Death. No one wanted to develop a close friendship with him. But the fine gentleman still remained kind. Whenever he was sent to take someone's soul, he would politely come and warn that person. Sometimes he even spared them and gave them a few extra days to become more prepared.

The old blacksmith, Yakuba, noticed the fine gentleman's kind behavior and, despite people's warnings, befriended him.

Those who were suspicious whispered, "If one does not enter the bush, he will not know what's in there. Yakuba has to learn a lesson."

From that time on, the fine gentleman Death would often come to visit his old friend Yakuba, have a chat and relax with him.

Years passed and Yakuba grew very old. It finally came time for Death to take his own best friend's soul back to his maker.

The day he appeared in Yakuba's shop with this news, the smith was very busy repairing many tools for the farmers of Sumamburu. The old smith Yakuba begged Death to spare his life for a few more days so he could finish sharpening all the tools.

The people watched the old smith working feverishly and sympathized with him.

"If Death does not kill him, this certainly will."

Two days later, Death returned to the old blacksmith's shop.

Yakuba begged again, "Please spare me for a few more hours! All these farmers' lives depend on the work I do! Without their farming tools, crops can't be grown and people will suffer."

Then he scrambled to clean a spot in the warmth of his shop for Death to rest a while.

The fine gentleman lay down so comfortably, he fell fast asleep. Every now and then he would stretch a leg there or an arm here until he accidentally hung his toe too close to the flames of Yakuba's fire.

Almost instantly he felt a sharp, burning pain traveling from his toe to his head. The scared Death quickly jumped up from his sleep and ran away at full speed, thinking that Yakuba the old smith was plotting to kill him.

When Death reached the Recipient of All Souls, he was terrified.

"Your majesty," he said, pointing to his burnt toe, "if you don't shield me from human sight, I am afraid they will kill me one day."

That was the last time Death was ever seen by anyone again.

Meanwhile, the old smith Yakuba who had proved his concern for the people of Sumamburu was pronounced their king. No one knew why Death had forgotten him, but he served as king for many enjoyable years.

✳

"See?" said Grandma. "It is natural to fear some things, but please don't be frightened forever."

Whether all these stories were based on real-life happenings or not, they certainly delivered messages with such gentleness that even a small child could learn from them.

For me, I learned something each time I heard one.

Knowledge

ONE DAY a rumor sprang up around town that new straw classrooms would be built. This made all the children in our compound excited.

Going to school was something that had been burning in my mind for a while, so I finally asked, "When can I go to school, Grandma?"

She paused and looked at me curiously. I guess she was wondering where this question had suddenly come from.

"All the children in the big city go to school," I added.

"Don't worry, Baba. You will go to school when you are educated," Grandma answered simply.

I was perplexed, wondering when that would be.

"Everyone says that one gains more knowledge by going to school."

Grandma responded with a big smile, showing her two deep dimples on the sides of her cheeks.

"Knowledge is everywhere around you, Baba. It can leap like a frog from one person to another, from a person to an animal, or from an animal to a person. But it's something you cannot see or capture like a butterfly or lizard. It

comes to you on one condition only — that you have the
desire for learning."

These words of Grandma made me even more anxious
about school, but I also understood it was time to quietly
follow her advice.

It was important to listen without a word of argument
and to respect the words of our elders, as they were our
consistent guides to life. No child was allowed "to put

mouth" into serious adult conversations without permission, or unless the situation was an emergency.

Even among the elders themselves, those who talked of current events were carefully chosen. They often used proverbs and metaphors to help make their talks enjoyable and make people think as they listened.

As the elders said, "In life, all things give birth to their own young except speech. Speech gives birth to its own mother. For a small misunderstood word can result in a huge war. It is sweet to be able to express your feelings with words, but once they are blown out from the mouth and into ears, it is impossible to retrieve them."

This is why only the experienced ones were chosen to deliver speeches, as they knew how to pick words thoughtfully so as not to ignite anger or disrespect.

A proverb from Mali says, "Having too much to say makes one an annoyance to others, but not having anything to say at all makes one fearful to others."

Or, "Words have layers like an onion. When you peel one, another will appear underneath."

Soon our sweet conversation was abruptly interrupted by the sudden buzzing sound of a twin-engine airplane flying high above our heads.

"Grandma, look! *Avion!*" I exclaimed as I squinted my almond eyes against the bright sun.

I pointed at the shiny airplane high in the sky, flying against the glare of the bright sunlight above.

Over the years, Grandma had recounted the story of the first airplane in the area. She had been young at the time, maybe between twenty-one and twenty-five rainy seasons old, when she and her girlfriends witnessed one of the very first airplanes that flew over Farafina (Africa).

"It flew its big belly over the landscapes of our region. It was amazing to see this huge jumping boat almost landing on the ground. But it was also the most frightening thing anyone had ever seen. From the top of the grassy hill we could see the European pilots dressed in khaki outfits. The propeller sounded *ching, ching, ching, ching*. Then blue smoke erupted from it and dust blew everywhere. The noise was so loud that everyone ran to hide in their huts."

"Grandma, what did the airplanes do?" I asked.

"They were celebrating the end of the war between France and Germany."

"Who won the war, Grandma?"

"France, but not without a huge effort from African soldiers," she responded.

"Grandma," I commented, "I wish I had been here in the village with you in those days. But it's fun to learn the stories from you also!"

Grandma responded mysteriously, "Yes, Baba. Just like it is impossible to live through Tuesday when it's only Monday. See all those trees and hills? Knowledge is older than them all, but it passes by those who are not listening or paying attention." She added, "Hear that smiling sun over there?" She pointed to the great orange African sun setting in the west, hanging over the hill behind the giant baobab trees.

"Yes, Grandma, but what is it saying?"

"It is whispering goodbye to us," Grandma replied. She wrapped her arms around my skinny shoulders as we walked toward home. "You are only ten rainy seasons old! You have lots of learning time ahead of you."

Slowly we made our way past our small river, Mobili-poni, and past Banamba, the large silk cotton tree at the entrance of the town. We stood on the old railroad tracks by our compound to watch the big orange sun drift behind the mountains of Kita.

In the end, the straw classrooms were built by the strong young men of the village. Unfortunately, they burned to the ground three times before the project was abandoned.

Nighttime

NIGHTTIME was beautiful. There was no electricity for light, but I liked the way the darkness forced me to use my senses and my experience to guide me.

It was fun to feel my way through the darkening night filled with noises. Bats, frogs, crickets, evening birds and dogs all chanted harmoniously like an orchestra. Sometimes we were blessed with light from bright stars and the occasional full moon that was enough to give shadow to an object.

Night was a true moment for relaxation. Unlike daytime, when laziness was not tolerated, night was the time when no one could be accused of being lazy.

After dinner, everyone would be present in the compound, seated in a circle around a wood fire waiting for Grandma's storytelling. Sometimes while we waited, we children would help our aunts shell a small bowl of peanuts for the next day's stew and entertain each other by retelling stories we had heard from the elders.

After a moment, Grandma would emerge from her room, carrying her beautifully carved wooden stool, a present she had received from Grandpa Samba's parents when they first married. She carefully placed the little wooden stool in its usual spot next to her favorite snack, a bowl full of steamed ngo-yo, African eggplant, to help digestion.

Once Grandma was seated, everyone would quiet down to show their respect and eagerness to hear her stories.

By now she was the oldest person in the compound. Grandpa had passed on mysteriously one afternoon after eating his lunch. He sat on his low chair leaning against the wall taking a nap as he had done forever. But that day, he sat napping from noon until Grandma returned in the evening and discovered that Grandpa Samba had passed on.

Grandma would clasp her hands together and begin, "We do not tell tales in daylight because that can bring misfortune upon us. But now is a good time to hear tales and learn from them.

"Brother Rabbit and Hyena..." she began, and would then explain in detail the position of each one of these characters in the traditional tales. Rabbit always played the role of a smart and crafty person! Hyena, on the other hand, always represented the foolish and dull, the one who gets in lots of trouble. These were the main two characters that helped children learn.

Of course, we children always preferred Rabbit.

"*N'tay, n'tay,*" she shouted proudly.

"*N'tay mansa,*" the children shouted back.

All her tales began this way. There was a reason for this.

Once, a sad and troubled king discovered the joy of storytelling. Stories became his therapy, clearing his mind and bringing happiness to his broken heart. But he did not understand that it was through sharing thoughts that stories were made. So he forced all the best storytellers in the kingdom into his royal courtyard and ordered them to tell and retell tales day and night for him alone to hear.

No storyteller could refuse the king. In fact, "No" became a forbidden word with severe punishment.

For a long time people could not tell or hear stories. They became tired of their greedy king's selfish behavior.

Eventually the people's hearts and minds were filled with sadness and anger, and together they taught the selfish king a lesson.

While he was sleeping in the same hammock he lay in to listen to stories, he was captured. The hammock was used to tie him in knots. Meanwhile, the people took stories back into their homes, and love and harmony into their kingdom.

As they say, "It is because of the people that one is called king, and it is because of the people that there is no king at all." People started to interrelate once again. One head alone cannot exchange ideas.

From that moment on, storytellers began their stories with the word that was once forbidden by the selfish king — *N'tay, n'tay,* meaning, "No, no." Children then respond, "*N'tay mansa,*" meaning, "No to the king," to symbolize their freedom.

After this call and response, Grandma Sabou would begin her stories. Each story was different. In the dark of the night she would tell each one with such seriousness, we would feel as if we were elements in her stories.

These stories, with their proverbs, metaphors and morals, would end the evening, giving everyone something to ponder as they went to sleep.

Stories were more than just a learning tool for my cousins and me. They were like going on an adventure.

Granary Boy

IN TIME, I was appointed caretaker of the family granaries. I was filled with pride to be given responsibility for the mouré, the measuring gourd.

My first duty each morning was to dispense the grain to my aunt Juma for the meals of the day. I would do this even before washing my face or finding a géssè stick to clean my teeth.

The granary was a tall cylindrical adobe hut built on stone stilts to prevent the grain from being damaged by insects and flood water. Inside, it was separated into four sections by low walls. A small window opening near the top of the granary could be reached by climbing a Y-shaped ladder.

One morning, after jumping into the granary, I heard a noise. I peered over the low wall and discovered a snake on the pile of garbanzo beans.

Trembling with fear, I called to my grandmother in a low voice, "Grandma, there is a snake here. It is the biggest and darkest serpent I have ever seen."

Calmly, Grandma climbed the forked ladder and peered through the narrow little entrance.

She paused momentarily and then said, "This is not a typical snake. This one can speak. We must not kill or harm this snake, for he is a messenger. He is telling us that someone is coming to visit us from far away. This is the person's shadow. If you kill the shadow, the person will cease to live."

So I slowly and quietly gathered the grain and climbed out of the granary.

Despite my grandmother's soothing words, I never stopped thinking about that serpent. Every time I passed the granary that day, I looked up at the door and thought of the big black serpent inside.

Later that evening, everyone was surprised by a new visitor. It was Penda, my own mother, whom I had not seen for a few years.

A neighbor and an old friend of the family named Numuké stood near me, leaning on his cane.

I looked up at him and said, "Grandma was really right about the serpent."

Numuké replied, "Maybe it is true what they say. A seated old woman can see farther than a standing young man. After all, have you ever seen a snake walk on four legs like a goat?"

"No," I replied quickly.

"That is because he is always crawling on his belly out of respect for others. We humans have a long way to go," said Numuké. He smiled with his one tooth and limped away to the foot of the old mango tree, where he watched me run to welcome my mother into the compound. Everyone cheered with happiness and spontaneously chanted joyful songs at her arrival.

In the evening, I crawled on the mat next to my mother to catch up after our many years of separation.

I couldn't wait to tell her about the serpent in the granary.

After Mama Penda patiently listened to my long explanation about the serpent, she said thoughtfully, "It takes a unique person to know the difference between a simple animal and the shadow of a human spirit. Your grandmother has this special knowledge. Hunters are considered to have special talents in divining, too. They were our first medicine men. They communed with wildlife to learn the secret mysteries of which herbs or plants were good for which illnesses. These animals are not simple snakes, antelope or buffalo. They are the spirits of the ancestors that come to hunters in the deepest moment of their divining.

"Not everyone can be a hunterman. But my father, Tumani, was one such hunter in his youth. His honesty through his divining and his generosity with his knowledge of healing helped the people in his village for many years. Whenever someone brought him a gift in exchange for his help, he would reject it, saying, 'My gifts are free.' However, the one reward that he could not reject was when the people began calling him Baba Wagué, Father of Trust. Eventually, his real name Tumani faded from everyone's mind and he became known only as Baba Wagué. This is where your name came from."

Even though I did not work as hard for my name, I was proud of my grandfather Baba Wagué, whom I was named after.

I then went on to tell Mama about the rest of the

happenings in the compound, and how Grandma Sabou was taking good care of us. Mama Penda smiled, looking at my face.

"Your grandma is special. Everyone loves her. There is no reward great enough to give to her for her efforts."

Nevertheless, Mama Penda went on and thanked Grandma Sabou in person for being a strong leaning rock for children. After that day, despite being still a little shaky about the serpent, I continued to fetch the grain from the granary, and I never saw the serpent again.

Washing Hands

AFTER MAMA Penda had settled in, she met with Grandma Sabou, Uncle Sumaïla and other elders in the compound to discuss when we boys must be seated, or circumcised. In our village, people referred to the circumcision initiation as "washing a child's hands."

"Don't you worry," she was told. "The time will come."

Uncle Sumaïla added, "As our crops did not do well this year, we are unable to undertake this ceremony."

Then Mama Penda announced, "My husband Abdoulaye and I had planned to do this before the children grew too old. Now that he is dead, we must respect his words. I came well prepared for these expenses."

"Then I yield to you, Penda. I know my brother — your husband — is no longer with us. But his words are here with us. It is said that speech lasts longer than its giver. This moment would have been special to my brother Abdoulaye."

Things then were quickly settled for three boys in the compound — myself and two of my cousins. A messenger was sent out to notify all the other families that had young boys in the village to join us if they could.

A week later, my two cousins and I were informed that we were old enough to have our hands washed, and that it would be taking place in just seven days.

Not knowing the true meaning of such words, we were quite excited. We had no idea what to expect, but to growing boys who were always hungry, washing hands meant only one thing — eating a lot of food!

Everyone waited patiently as the preparation for the ceremony slowly unfolded, growing bigger and bigger. Hundreds of kilos of green millet were delivered for the delicious traditional millet cake called day-gay. Four well-fed sheep were brought from a neighboring town into the compound.

When the actual day came for the hand washing, all of us boys were brought together in one place. We all knew each other, for we had played together in the dirt as young children for many years.

By sunset that evening, the celebration had begun with drumbeats and mothers gathering together. Of course, this meant nearly all the women in the village. They began to pound the green millet into flour, chopping vegetables, cutting meat, chanting happy songs as they played water drums. The hand-clapping sounds could be heard far away to draw more people.

However, we boys were kept secluded in a big adobe room far away from all these sights. We sang songs to entertain ourselves while we waited.

When the food was ready, they brought our part to us.

It was divine. Everyone washed their hands well and we ate way beyond our limits. Out in the compound, they had already finished eating and the ceremony reached its peak

with the Sogonikun masked dancers. From the small windows of our room, we could see them dancing to the drumbeats in the moonlight.

We waited for a long time. At ten o'clock, no one had yet come to see us. By eleven o'clock, we began to have the feeling that maybe there was more to washing hands than just eating.

Soon midnight arrived with the barking of roaming dogs in the narrow streets of the village. It was now the real moment of truth.

Uncle Sumaïla came with an older man named Shaka. He introduced him to us as our zayma, or supervisor. Shaka then began to put us in line one after another, depending on how old we were. We were each given a simple, deep yellow robe that reached all the way to our ankles. I noticed that no pants came with the robe and became a little more suspicious.

"How strange to have a top made for boys without pants?" I commented. But no one around me paid attention, so I gave up and waited patiently to see what would happen next.

Soon Shaka guided us into a long line. Then we followed each other, walking through the main street, crossing the entire town in the darkest of night, making our way to the western end of the village. We passed the empty market square, the house of the village chief, and the last living quarter of the town.

There were no sounds, not even a breath of wind. The sound of drumbeats far from my home compound could be heard at this end of the town.

In ordinary circumstances, we would never have dared to venture into these areas of the town. The only place that we had not yet passed was the lonely single clinic house a half mile from town where Bourama, the only doctor, and the town blacksmith worked together.

"There is a light in the clinic," we whispered to each other. When we finally reached the entrance, Bourama threw open the door and welcomed us brusquely.

Upon entering the clinic, we were taken into a large room with long benches. We were instructed to sit down in line and wait, facing a wall with large posters of syringes advertising the importance of inoculations.

A moment later, each boy was called and one by one taken into a small chamber where the real hand washing took place. Some screamed and some only shed tears, but I knew that this was our bridge to manhood.

In the end, all of us were brave and were considered heroes. We were now initiated, graduating from one part of society to a higher level.

After the initiation, we began our journey back into town. Shuffling along, wearing our new yellow robes pulled tautly away from our torsos, we waddled like penguins, legs apart. We passed the chief's house and crossed the large empty marketplace, slowly making our way home through the dark night to the big room that was called the buray. This room would be our healing place.

When we finally arrived, we found the room well decorated. Each boy's mother had brought him a new mat, pillow and blanket. As the celebration for our families continued through the rest of the night, we boys began our fragile and restless sleep lying stiffly on our backs.

We lived this solitary lifestyle for four weeks, only seeing the outside when the morning sunlight glared through the high windows of the buray. Shaka watched over us all day long, and Uncle Sumaïla became the zayma at night.

After a week, the intense pain slowly decreased, and we boys began to feel like ourselves physically and mentally. From that moment on, we could walk independently to the bathroom, but we spent most of the day sitting with our backs against the wall as our zayma taught us the many traditional circumcision songs for hours. This would shift our minds away from the constant minor irritations and help us to recover more quickly.

Within three weeks, we had learned more than forty songs. Many young men remembered these songs all of their lives.

At the end of three weeks, we boys were led by our zayma on a long field trip to the river outside the village. There they bathed us carefully to prevent water from touching our healing wounds.

In the evening we marched back to our buray chanting our heroic songs. We each had a shaker carved from old gourds. As we shook those shakers, we sang songs comparing ourselves to eagles that fly high above all, masters of the sky, the ones that look down over others.

We had reached manhood. Now it was the time to watch over those who had cared for us.

As we came closer to the village, our zayma merged the song into a new rhythm: "When we went to the river, the

water was untouchably hot. We saw nothing but one lonely red-tailed bawfaro, the mermaid on the banks. But when we reached home, home was sweet and fresh."

I thought, "Why are we singing like this, as the river just gave us plenty of refreshment?" But I soon realized the song was just a metaphor, saying there is no place like home, as we were welcomed by a colorful crowd of our mothers dressed in their best, holding giant bowls of delicious food.

By the end of the fourth week, we were almost completely healed. We could even run and jump a little. We played a game called dugadaw by putting precious objects on the road to trick those who can't pass anything they see on the ground. Then we would hide ourselves in an old house or behind a ruined wall as we watched carefully. When some unsuspecting person would pick up the precious item, we would storm out from all directions, shaking our gourd shakers wildly and loudly and chanting, following that individual around. Sometimes we would follow them all the way to their homes until we not only got our precious item back, but were also rewarded with either grain or money.

This was truly annoying to some people, but no one could dare complain, as it had been the tradition for generations.

At the end of this final week, the zaymas delivered the boys back to their homes as young men. The grain and money we had collected would now be used for the closing ceremony.

At dawn, the mothers formed a large circle, waving woven grass fans in the air and chanting the songs "Layfa laa yelay" and "Denko." They sang to the world that their children were everything that held them together, and that if they had to die, they would die for their children.

I had never felt such pride as that day, as I watched my mother among the women.

Mama Penda

MAMA PENDA stayed in the village for another whole month. She shared with us children many of her special proverbs.

Everyone learned something from her. We all thought of her as a good philosopher because her messages were always so unusual. People waited anxiously to hear what she had to say.

This could have been because Mama Penda was from a different ethnic group, the Soninke, and she was very traditional in the way she spoke. She routinely awakened others with old forgotten phrases that often cracked us into laughter.

"How do these old sayings still come to you so easily?" some asked curiously.

Mama Penda would respond, "These are words that come from the tongues of my elders. I was born into them and have spoken like this since I was very young like you. But now I don't have to think too hard. They just feed themselves into my mind."

For example, one time she saw a boy named Baru

mercilessly kicking a freshly built termite hill, sending termites scurrying in all directions.

She paused and said, "Destroying others greatly diminishes your own chance for harbor." As the boy stared at her she continued, "After all, we have the same soul, in spite of our differences in size."

One afternoon in the compound, she caught some soccer-hungry boys picking unripe mangoes and kicking them around as soccer balls.

Again she paused and said, "Boys, don't waste the babies of that tree. She is a mother just like me."

Everyone found Mama Penda's messages curiously unusual. Her visit in the village was both educational and entertaining, and people later laughed warmly whenever they thought of her.

My encounter with my mother was even more educational. I learned the names of several other trees on the home farm that carried the names of relatives who had planted them.

When I forgot the name of one of the trees, Mama Penda would jog my memory.

"This is Badambow."

"How do you know the names of all these trees?" I asked my mother.

Mama Penda replied, "Your father and I lived here when we first married. I knew most of those people that the mango trees are now named after."

Later on, Mama Penda and I took a short walk to Sinzamba, an area directly connected to the compound and fenced with mugubagani bushes, where Uncle Sumaïla grew sugar cane and sweet corn. But the land also had a few mango trees.

"What do you think the name of this tree is?" my mother asked me, her right hand pressed to the trunk. "That's me, Baba! This tree is named Penda."

I looked my mother in the eyes, smiling, wishing I had known that a long time ago.

"Good Mama, your own tree! Now I understand why you say the tree is a mother just like you." After telling me the names of the other trees, we moved toward the low gravel hills that separated our lands from other properties.

Mama Penda climbed a hill, squinting as she gazed deeply toward an old gravel dune at the western edge of our compound.

"Mama, it's an old railway," I shouted at her.

"I know, Baba. This makes me think of the good days when your father Abdoulaye was an industrial engineer. He also worked with the railway company training young train conductors."

I knew this was not easy for Mama Penda. I only vaguely remembered my father, but everyone in the village talked about his kindness and his generosity.

One time Grandma commented about the same old gravel dune, "This is where your father Abdoulaye used to conduct the train past the village. Whenever the train passed by here, we carefully listened for the whistle. His siblings would run waving hands and shouting greetings. At other times, he would drop goods he had brought for us. During his time as a conductor, he earned good money and lavished many gifts on his brothers — farming tools,

donkey carts, sewing machines, herds of goats and sheep —
— all for the family."

As Grandpa had said, "Each child is like a day of the
week. Each of them is special, just as Monday cannot be
Tuesday. Abdoulaye did many good things as a young
man."

✳

GRANDPA SAMBA was so proud of my father Abdoulaye
that he decided to find a good wife for him. So he traveled
to the neighboring town of Wassala to see a well-respected
man called Tumani, to ask for the hand of his daughter for
his son. This was how Mama Penda and Papa Abdoulaye met.

Fortunately, the two of them liked each other, and the
ceremony was held soon after that. But during the ceremony, Papa Abdoulaye recognized a familiar person in the
crowd. He knew he had not invited him. The man was one
of the many young men he had trained for the railway
years ago.

The young man was Lanzenu, the direct brother of his
new wife Penda. The joy of that big surprise to Papa
Abdoulaye really sweetened the day of their wedding.

Papa Abdoulaye continued his job with the railroad
while Mama Penda lived with his parents in Kassaro for a
while.

In the end, good luck came upon them when Papa
Abdoulaye got a new position in the Socoma factory in the
town of Baguinda near Bamako. They moved there together, and my two brothers, two sisters and I were all born.

But just before my younger sister was born, Papa Abdoulaye's life was suddenly cut short in an accident. As my people put it, he had returned to his new home.

*

EVEN THOUGH I had already learned much since I had come to the village, Mama Penda was definitely a different kind of influence, and my growing boy's ears itched to hear more of her stories.

She said that trees are the symbol of life because each leaf symbolizes a person or a living creature, and these are the same people or creatures you meet in life. Those are your neighbors on the branches of trees. So this is why it is important to pay attention, to respect and to be kind to others, because they help make up who you are.

"Well, what about genies and spirits that we can't even see?" I asked.

Mama Penda chuckled and said, "You just want to know it all, don't you? See, young man, the world is only one thing, and everything that exists in it is made out of it. This means we are all part of one another."

"But why are genies and spirits invisible?" I asked.

"Eeeh," said Mama Penda, "sometimes even the tongue and the teeth quarrel in the mouth. One cannot know about all the things that happen. That is why the world is a mysterious place. I will tell you a story."

*

ONCE, A FARMER *was working hard to clear a field for his farm. Exhausted and thirsty, he sat in the shade to rest and quench his thirst, when suddenly he was interrupted by the voice of a genie.*

"Why are you cultivating my land without my permission?"

The farmer turned around and, upon seeing the genie, he politely apologized for unknowingly working his land.

Meanwhile, the crafty genie was standing in the middle of the bean field admiring the beautiful green leaves of the beans.

"What a wonderful field of peanuts," commented the genie, who had never seen bean plants before. Even though the land was not really his, the genie went on to propose a deal with the farmer.

"If you agree to let me keep the bottom parts of the peanut plants while you take the top parts, I will let you continue to use my land."

The farmer understood the treachery of arguing with a genie and, knowing that the field grew beans instead of peanuts, he quickly agreed.

The genie looked at the beautiful green field and was content that he had fooled a human.

"When all these peanuts are ready, I am sure to be rich," he said to himself.

But at harvest, the farmer collected all of his beans and sold them in the market.

The genie, on the other hand, pulled up the remainder of the bean plants — roots, dirt and all — and took all

this to the marketplace to sell. People looked at him strangely and ignored him. He sold not a single leaf.

The genie realized he had made a mistake and decided to try his trick on the farmer the next season.

The following year, he was quick to claim the top part of whatever the farmer was going to grow. But the clever farmer then planted potatoes, and when harvest time arrived, the genie again collected all the leaves and stems while the farmer dug out the potatoes and sold them in the market.

This time, people pointed fingers and laughed at the genie.

The genie became furious and said, "Those humans are much too clever."

With that, he mysteriously disappeared from sight, and his kind was never seen again.

He learned that tricking other beings only ruins a potentially good partnership: "If you throw dust in the eyes of your playmate, you will be enjoying loneliness for a while."

As for the farmer, he kept on alternating his crop each year, and the harvest continued to get better and better.

Rainy Season

WHEN MAMA Penda left the village, she had one more question for Grandma Sabou and Uncle Sumaïla.

"When will the children go to school?"

"School?" they responded. "Oh, no. It spoils the children and makes them forget their roots. They are learning plenty of things right here in the village."

"But they still must go to school," Mama Penda insisted.

"We should not want them to grow up torturing others. Or should we?" Grandma replied, referring to the colonial times.

"I understand that, Mother Sabou, but shouldn't the children know at least how to write their own names?" Mama Penda asked.

In the end an agreement was made, but Grandma Sabou pleaded with Mama Penda to be patient until my brothers and I had finished our "village" education.

As she always put it, "They cannot go to school until they are educated!"

✳

GRANDMA SABOU and Uncle Sumaïla gave excellent guidance to all of us children, but Mama Penda left some special gifts in everyone's hearts and minds. We were all sad to see her go. For quite some time, whenever a small problem would sprout in the compound, someone would be quick to say, "Mama Penda could solve that."

As for myself, knowing about that mango tree named after Mama Penda made village life more special. It was no longer just the place where my father was born and grew up, but a place that symbolized my mother, too. Whenever I missed Mama Penda, I would run to that mango tree and give her a great big old hug.

Mama Penda left at a good time. It was early June and the rain clouds darkened the sky daily. Farmers began preparing their lands.

As the farm work increased, the compound became quieter. Most of the adults and bigger children spent the entire day in the field. I was old enough now to join the older children on the farm after tending the goats and sheep in the morning.

Sometimes the dark clouds quickly gathered from full bright sunlight, turning the day into night for several hours. The loud sound of thunder followed, scary as a grouchy savannah lion roaring to defend his territory. Lightning cracked the sky open, as if that sleeping lion had just opened his eyes and blinked, lighting up the whole world.

The rain fell, pounding hard against the dry landscape like herds of elephants stamping *gueep, gueep, gueep* to the far reaches of the land. Instantly the dry crackly land turned wet and moist, waking up all the sleeping creatures.

First, millions of termites emerged out of the ground, flapping their wings and flying all over in a low cloud. Next came the birds to feed off the termites. After a little while many termites lost their wings and dropped to the ground,

inviting an army of frogs, toads and lizards to swallow them up. Some snakes even showed up.

This chaotic and lively event took place within the first few rainstorms of the year. In the end the land turned green, and the orangish earth looked clean and smelled good with its many beautiful plants, flowers and colorful insects. The presence of the banikono birds indicated the season would be abundant.

Mobili-poni, our small river, would flood its banks, dividing the village in two. Children would wander up and down its sandy banks, watching the birds catch fish in the bumpy, fast-running water.

Sometimes my friends and I would hang out there to catch sand crabs to race. Even though these sand crabs came from fresh water and were smaller than their cousins in the sea, they still gave painful pinches. We would tie their claws with small, hefty vines, and after we had each captured three or four, we would find a nice dry spot on the hill to put our crabs to race. The winner would collect a pile of fruit or nuts.

But it was not an easy game to play, as crabs are even more stubborn than donkeys. They would scatter in all directions, crawling sideways into grassy thickets.

At the end of the game, we took the crabs back to the river, watching them dig holes through the sand to find their way to water. We would then scurry home ourselves, before the next thunderstorm began.

The Chibow

I WAS OFTEN frightened by the long and everlasting lightning and thunder that would move noisily across the almost treeless savannah around the village. The loud thunder always drove children and women inside their homes, their hearts pounding. But the rainy season was also a great time of the year when the young did the chibow — community farm work. Numukeba, the town blacksmith, would sharpen old tools for the farmers.

Usually smith work is a family trade. In the tradition, only someone whose father was a smith could be one also.

But Numukeba did not come from a family of smiths.

His real name was Lassana Coulibaly, and he was born into a traditional Bambara farming family. But after many years of drought, he ran away from his native Bambara land in search of new opportunities.

In the west, miles away from his native village, Lassana found a new home and new life. He built himself a small hut for a workshop. There he mended old farming tools for the village people.

In a few years, his talents were so well known that the

village people gave him the name Numukeba — the Great Blacksmith. Children competed for the privilege to deliver a tool to Numukeba for mending. He was always cheerful, and he sang his words when he talked to the children. They loved him.

Numukeba had many years of success and earned large sums of money. He married a young woman from the village and together they had some children. Numukeba was truly prosperous, and he felt that this was where his heart belonged.

But it is also said, "No matter how long an old log remains in the river, it will never turn into a crocodile."

One day, a woman called Tata, one of the wealthiest farmers in the region, approached Numukeba to sharpen all of her tools for a chibow on her farm which was to take place in one week. This great festivity required many tools for the many young men and women working together to prepare the earth for planting. People from all over the region were gathering for this work party in her fields.

Numukeba, knowing the greatness of Tata, decided it would be better if he did the work instead of his apprentices.

He worked day and night, sharpening the tools slowly and surely.

Every time Tata visited the workshop, she furrowed her brow and urged Numukeba to work faster. Tata was a woman of power, and many lives depended on her success in the region. She started mumbling, then shouting, and finally she began complaining about Numukeba.

Soon gossip sprang up around town, and some people of the village began to turn against him.

Some said, "He shouldn't have even been allowed to be a blacksmith."

Others said, "Let us have him return to his native place. He does not belong in our village."

However, Numukeba was a courageous man with a good heart. Most important, it was his funny sense of humor that attracted many people to him. Even though he knew he was not a smith by family trade, he was still committed to this profession and had proudly performed it for many years. Numukeba knew there were others who would like to change their livelihoods as he had done, but they were not courageous enough to do so.

One day Numukeba picked up a small tamani drum, placed it under his arm and began to play on it and sing a sweet song. It was his way to express himself and also give a message to Tata and all the other people who had tried to put him down.

> *Eeeh, Tata, ko mandi bela, ko mandi mogo la, ko mandi bela.*
> Hey, Tata, tradition is not good for everyone. One must learn and move beyond one's tradition.

> *Ne don na kalan na, ne dona avion boli kalan na. Avion boli madia n'na.*
> You see, I tried to learn how to fly an airplane, but found that it was not for me.

> *Ne don na kalan na, ne dona taxi boli la. Taxi boli madia n'na.*

I became a taxi driver. It was not a success for me.

Ne don na kalan na, ne ye sene kalan ke. Sene madia n'na.
I was once a farmer and things did not sprout for me.

*Ne don na kalan na, ne dona jagoke kalan na. Jago kalan
madia n'na.*
I learned to be a trader, but I earned no gold.

*Kana ne bila numu ya baara la, numu ya baara diara
n'na.*
Finally I turned to becoming a blacksmith, where I
bent metal and carved wood.

*Eeeh, Tata, ko mandi bela, ko mandi mogo la, ko mandi
bela.*
Hey, Tata, one must not struggle doing something
that is not worth struggling for. The smith job is
good work for me.

Numukeba sang this song, walking through every narrow street of town. He was soon joined by his steadfast
friends, the children.

As they walked the streets, clapping and cheering, the
people began to listen to Numukeba's message of personal
freedom.

When the day of the chibow arrived, Numukeba gra-
ciously delivered all of Tata's tools, well mended and sharp-
ened. The men with their tools, gleaming in the bright
sunlight, moved in harmony across the fields, cutting the

earth in time to the music of drums and balafons. Women cheered the men on, offering gourds of water and the promise of food after their tiring work.

Tata smiled. Her chibow was a success. Her smile soon floated over to Numukeba and planted itself on his face.

"So much gold, so much silver, but only friendship holds the true meaning of wealth," Tata said.

Numukeba had regained Tata's trust and respect. This is how he was able to make a change in his little corner of the world. His song changed the hearts and minds of many people in the village and throughout the region. His nickname became Banumukeba, meaning, Father, the Great Smith.

Numukeba knew that being true to yourself was a sure way to know your true friends. His story was an inspiration for the whole town, particularly for my family, who had befriended and hosted him when he first arrived in the village.

Family History

WHEN I ASKED my grandma, "How did our family make it here?" she paused for a moment, knowing that only the oral historians are qualified to narrate histories.

Many people don't understand the difference between storytellers of oral history and folktales. But they are very different.

In Mali, oral history is reserved for a special class of storytellers called djeliw, or bards. These people are the descendants of those who were the powerful and honored advisors and masters of speech for the past kings of Africa. The kings treated these storytellers with much respect, as they were essentially the libraries of the kingdom.

This is the same role that djeliw still play in Mali today, except there are no longer kings to reward them. The oral historians still practice the ancient customs of their forefathers at weddings, naming ceremonies and other celebrations.

Folktales play a different role in the function of the society. They are like narrative versions of metaphors or proverbs, used both to entertain and to teach. They reveal

respect for ourselves, for others, and for the relationships between man and nature. Folktales are also passed on from generation to generation and are told by anyone regardless of their ethnicity or background. Telling folktales in my family was important because we were a big farming family.

Grandma Sabou tried her best to answer, telling me what she knew of the family history: "Our relatives originally came from right here in the Fuladugu area. We are the Fulani of Wassolon, the owners of livestock. But with time we changed our ways. To survive, we turned to farming as well — just like Numukeba chose to change."

Grandma continued, "There once lived a Mandinka emperor named Samory Touré. He was a powerful man and had a large number of Sofa warriors known throughout the land for their recklessness. The mighty king and his Sofa often abused smaller and less powerful kingdoms, stealing young men to empower his own kingdom. His reckless actions made him unpopular in the region.

"However, when Europeans began to control many lands in West Africa, Samory had the best idea of uniting with his African brothers. His goal was to unify all the great leaders to form a powerful resistance army to block the progress of French colonization. He tried to put his past behind him and make peace with his neighbors.

"But his mission was taken as simple propaganda to take control. Samory gained ground, however, with a few strong individual believers who followed him wherever he went, including some of our ancestors. It was a bumpy ride moving from camp to camp, hiding from the French colonialists. The mighty king's food bank weakened, he lost many warriors and soon there was no blacksmith to make weapons. Then the Sofa army became frail, leaving Samory on the run alone with a handful of men to protect him.

"Inevitably, Samory was captured by the French and deported to Gabon where he died in 1900. But it was said that through his strategy, our people expanded to the eastern part of Mali," Grandma finished.

Slingshots

THE VILLAGE had been sweet to me, and each thing I learned about it made it even more special. We children were not always perfect, but we were happy because we had plenty of time to play and build our own toys. We twined sticks together to make little cars and carved wheels out of broken gourds.

But my favorite toy of all was an old donkey cart wheel that was given to me by our neighbor. On market days I would roll it along the dusty, snaky streets of the village, waving at friends and weaving around slow-moving women carrying baskets on their heads.

The smell of the village changed that day, as everyone left their work on the farms to sell their goods in the market. Young men on their bicycles with bags of spices tied behind, donkey carts piled high with sugar cane or grain, women frying bean cakes and sweet potatoes added to the excitement of the day.

But at the same time, village life could also be challenging and fearful. One day after a big rain storm, my cousins and I went out exploring the river as we always did following a storm, to help free soaking wet birds trapped under the bushes.

We suddenly noticed something unusual floating on the surface of the water.

It looked like a pink inner tube.

"Inner tube! Inner tube!" we shouted.

Jaygui, my oldest cousin who was deaf and mute, made his usual loud growling sound running toward it, and all of us followed him into the knee-deep water.

An inner tube was a valuable thing for boys, because we could slice it with a razor blade into fine strips for slingshot rubber. Every young boy fashioned his own slingshot to wear proudly around his neck. We always had a pocket full of stones at the ready to practice our marksmanship.

But when we came closer to this pink inner tube floating on the water, we were stunned at a transformation that was taking place right before our eyes.

The inner tube was a hungry albino cobra snake that had been holding onto its own tail to deceive prey. The snake slowly unfolded itself and straightened for a moment before wriggling and diving into the blurry red water of the river.

We quickly turned and ran for our lives, pumping our legs as fast as possible to escape the snake. When we finally made it to shore, everyone was exhausted, but we managed to make it to the high land, making sure the snake wasn't following us.

Only then did we realize that we had crossed the river and were on the opposite bank from our home. None of us were willing to put a foot into that water again to cross back to the village.

Finally we decided to make our way up the hill to the old colonial train station.

With the first light of day, we got up and sneaked back home using a little side road that went into the compound.

Unfortunately, we walked straight into Uncle Sumaïla. He was relieved to see us safely at home, but nothing could have saved us from the huge trouble we all feared from our uncle.

Thanks to Numukeba, who walked into the compound that morning, we were spared our uncle's wrath. Because of the blacksmith's intervention, we were simply given extra daily chores.

Jaygui

THE CHORES for us children increased a little after that incident.

The days I always looked forward to were the ones when I trained my younger cousins how to herd sheep and goats. This was fun and exciting, but it was also a challenging responsibility for me.

First they had to learn the skills of survival in the bush by identifying varieties of wild fruits, nuts and roots, as the edible foods had poisonous cousins on the same land. They also had to locate and remember all the watering holes in the area and the good resting spots for their herds.

Most important, the boys had to learn about the wild animals and how to get along with them. We would often be confronted by hungry animals such as baboons, porcupines, snakes, wild dogs and birds that depended on the same sources of food.

Despite all the risks, I taught my cousins to use their good sense, mind their own safety first and to remember what they learned from the many stories they were told. We took the necessary precautions but learned to share the food with these creatures.

Each day that passed brought new discoveries and new experiences to our lives in the grassland. The presence or absence of certain animals forecast the seasons' changes. This told us when and where to move our herds. The rocks and termite mounds became our guides to different areas. When I recognized my landmark friends, I would feel at home once more.

This was how I began to understand the importance of nature and sharing our world with the other creatures that live with us.

At sunset after a long day, my cousins and I and our well-fed goats would slowly head back to the village. Sometimes we met other villagers at the crossroads coming from their farms. Some people carried tall bales of hay and others rode on the backs of their donkeys.

We would exchange greetings — "*Aw kamalen*. You and youthfulness."

We boys would proudly answer back, "*M'ba, I ni baara*. Yes, you and hard work."

Once at home, we would put the goats in their night house and draw some water from the well to take a bucket bath. Soon after that, everyone would be present in the compound for the evening meal. In the darkening hours, stories would be told around an open fire.

August is the month of celebration because it is the time when all the crops should be ready. Harvest festivals happen all over the place. Shepherds do not need to herd sheep and goats at this time, as there is plenty of fodder around for the animals to eat.

As harvest drew closer, my young cousins and I were

needed to join our older cousins to help with the farm's harvest.

Jaygui was the oldest of all the boys. Therefore, we all had to obey his orders. He could not talk or hear, but he could growl like a wild lion. His life had been brushed by meningitis disease when he was younger, which also left him slightly paralyzed in one leg. He had a bad temper, and the looks he could give with his large round eyeballs were seriously frightening.

None of us young cousins would dare be foolish enough to offend him.

But underneath all that, Jaygui was a smart and talented musician like his father. His favorite instrument was the soku, the African version of a violin made with a small gourd, a stick and horse-tail hairs.

When he played, Jaygui would sit against the trunk of a tree and press the gourd part of his horse-tail violin on his lap. Next he gripped his lower lip with his upper smiling teeth. Then he slowly lowered his eyelids to cover his big round eyeballs and diligently began to play the violin, moving his head up and down, then from side to side, as if he could hear his own tunes.

It was mysterious, but its sweet and nostalgic sounds put people to sleep like pets. It made me believe the old saying, "The sweet sound of the horse-tail violin was meant for the spirits, but it is also not taboo for humans."

If one could have compared its sound to a taste, it would be the taste of honey.

At this precious moment no one could guess that Jaygui was a deaf or mute person, as he had so much control of his

soku. He was respected not only because he was the oldest boy among us, but because he was an unusually talented musician.

One afternoon, after hours of hard work in the garbanzo bean fields under the glaring sun, lunch arrived. We gathered together under the big lengay tree to eat, when suddenly we spotted a white man coming in our direction.

Everyone was surprised, since Europeans rarely passed by this part of the country.

When the stranger reached us sitting in the shade, he

threw his old beat-up backpack to the ground, then pulled a dark blue striped handkerchief from his back pocket to wipe sweat and red dust from his face. He then raised his two hands up in the air to greet us.

Cousin Jaygui, the oldest, patted the ground next to him, indicating to the guest that he was welcome and could now sit down.

None of us could tell the nationality of this strange man as we could speak nothing but Bambara, our native language. It didn't really matter, because we could communicate very well with random hand gestures as we had been doing with cousin Jaygui.

We waved our hands to indicate "Come to eat," inviting the stranger to join us.

Instead, the guest opened his large bag loaded with strange noisy things and pulled out a small hard plastic bowl. He held it up to Jaygui, who filled it with cooked beans. He then sat next to us in the shade as we ate and enjoyed the peacefulness of the moment.

But a moment later, Jaygui unexpectedly began to behave in a strange manner. Peering steadily into the gray sky far away, he abruptly stood up. He looked left, then right, and then began to run as fast as he could into the woods, like a donkey bitten by a hornet.

He looked as if he had gone mad, leaving everyone sitting in a state of wonder.

While the rest of us stared at each other, not able to make sense of what was going on, we were suddenly awakened to a noisy, fast-moving dark cloud careening toward us.

An army of African honey bees! The bees sounded like a crowd of humans loudly mumbling in the distance.

The whole wide forest land suddenly appeared to be a small space with no hiding places for us.

My older brother Samba hopped on the back of a family donkey called Ballablen. At first the stubborn donkey took him on a wild tour toward the cloud of bees and then took many U-turns, finally taking him into the thorny bushes.

My cousins and I were worried as we raced away on foot, leaving Samba and stubborn Ballablen to continue their lurching dance.

Ultimately, everyone ended up heading in the direction we knew best — the road leading to town. As we regrouped and redoubled our efforts to flee the bees, Samba and his donkey unexpectedly flew by with hooves raising dustballs in the air and hind legs kicking, braying loudly like a disabled old engine.

Suddenly, the beast bucked brother Samba off his back, throwing him high into the air. Luckily he landed on a soft bed of sand in the middle of the road. Everyone scrambled to help him up, but his body was totally covered with thorns from the wild ride, so he ducked beneath a small thicket by the road for shelter.

The rest of us continued our run toward town. Ballablen the donkey disappeared from our view as he galloped away on the winding road.

As for the European man, we only saw him running straight into the town's sacred forest, a place where even the native people had never been. It was a thick, dark and

deep forest with all sorts of dangerous creatures. The area was only about a square kilometer in size. The earlier villagers believed that a long time ago, this was the home of a large cow-sized bird that was capable of swallowing any human being who dared to cross into its space.

When we reached the village, we reported the news of the European's run into the sacred forest to the elders. Such news traveled fast across the entire town, with people shouting in all directions, "The giant bird has eaten a white man."

Some people remembered the very same European man in town earlier that day, speaking Portuguese. Almost instantly the song and rhythm changed — "The bird has swallowed a Portuguese man."

Twenty to thirty men, young and old, marched around the edge of the sacred forest shouting the only name they knew for the stranger — "Portugais, Portugais, Portugais?"

But no one answered. People looked for the Portuguese's hat, his shoes and his bag, but there were no signs of these things to be found.

In the end, it was believed that the Portuguese guy had been swallowed by the cow-sized bird. A little ceremony was held in memory of him and his disappearance.

However, a handful of people believed the stranger simply continued on his journey. That story ended as mysteriously as it had begun.

Finally the harvest was finished and there would be no farm work until the next rainy season in May.

During this time we youngsters spent much of our time training and racing donkeys and sometimes making our own toys. But I also remembered that it had been more than a year since Mama Penda had visited the village, and I missed her.

So I said to Grandma, "I really, really want to go to school."

I was hoping I would be sent to Mama in the city.

The City

MY PRAYER was answered one morning with a big surprise.

As I was readying my goats for the grasslands, I looked up and saw Uncle Sumaïla, well dressed, going toward Grandma's house.

"Baba, come here!" Sumaïla shouted. "You're not herding goats today."

"What is it, Uncle Sumaïla?"

Coming closer, he gently replied, "I'm going to Bamako where your mother lives. She sent a message asking my permission to return you while you still have a chance to go to French school. But first we must talk to Grandma about it."

Together we slowly walked around the walls of the huts to Grandma's place at the corner.

After exchanging the respectful formal greetings, we patiently listened to the lists of benedictions from Grandma. Uncle Sumaïla and I responded, "*Amiin,*" after each one.

After a short moment of quietness, Uncle Sumaïla handed Grandma a few cola nuts rolled in fresh leaves.

When he explained my mother's mission, I felt suddenly saddened. I wrapped myself up in the warm folds of my
grandmother's boubou dress. It was a bittersweet moment
for both of us.

But Grandma Sabou knew that I was wise enough to go
back to my mother. She leaned over and stroked my head
with her right hand.

"You are ready, Baba. You have achieved your tasks in
the village. You must go on now and learn more from
schoolteachers and the rest of the world. But remember,
we will always be best friends. I will visit you as often as I
can."

I looked up into the eyes of my grandmother and asked,
"When?"

"Soon enough, I promise. After all, your father was my
son, too."

Grandma softly grabbed hold of my hand and gently
pulled me into her room as Uncle Sumaïla waited outside.
We sat on the metal iron bed that my father had made.

Then she said, "Baba, always remember the road you
traveled on."

"I've heard that before," I thought. "It means your
future comes from your past."

After that, she opened up her wooden trunk to retrieve
an old multi-colored headscarf from her youth. I helped
her to spread it flat on the ground, then folded the few
clothes I owned. Grandma tied them in a bundle and put
them on the bed next to us as we quickly filled up a small
plastic bag with fresh peanuts — a present for my mother.

When we came out, Uncle Sumaïla was patiently waiting.

"We'd better get going, Baba. We do not want to miss the early morning train."

But before we rushed out, Grandma Sabou quickly recited a few words of blessing.

"May you pass all the tests of life, may you make peace with anyone you meet, and may you rise high like a bird."

Uncle Sumaïla and I held our fingertips on our foreheads, responding, "*Amiin*, amen, amen."

We then began our walk to the train stop, about thirty minutes away.

When we reached the station, Uncle Sumaïla went to pay for his ticket at a crowded little window as I watched over the baggage by the railroad tracks. I did not need to pay, for children younger than eighteen were free.

I was excited but a little scared. So Uncle Sumaïla comforted me by saying, "Trains won't buck you off like a donkey — just kidding. Trains are fun."

Although it is true the making of the railway was one of the few good things left by French colonialists, all the hard labor was done by Africans. It is the main link from the Atlantic Ocean in the west to the upper Niger delta in the northeast.

As we waited, the whistling of the train could be heard at a distance, sliding through the rocky outcroppings in the west. A loud engine noise shattered the air, and dark blue smoke rose, hiding the entire train. A horn sounded to announce the arrival of the old locomotive at the station.

I had never been so close to a train before.

"Where is it? Where is the train?" I wondered.

Uncle Sumaïla pointed to the dusty cloud. But all I saw

was blue smoke, red dust and dry leaves flying in the air. Women's scarves were blown from their heads, and chickens squawked and fluttered away. I heard the screeching sound of the brakes. It was frightening.

When the dust settled, the beautiful green, yellow and red striped engine became visible. The train slowed and the screeching sound ended.

I held tightly to Uncle Sumaïla. As the train came to a complete stop, he quickly grabbed the baggage and threw it onto the deck of the train. He scrambled up with the help of two metal bars. Then he pulled me up by my two skinny arms.

Inside, there weren't any seats available and barely a place to stand. We sat on bags of millet piled high in the aisle.

After a short moment, the train honked to warn of its departure. As it pulled slowly away from the station, I waved goodbye to the crowd of village people who waved back, shouting their farewells.

Since it was my first train ride, I was very curious, looking up and down and out the window. The trees, donkey carts and women carrying firewood all swirled quickly away from my view.

The train was packed with travelers — tourists, merchant men and women, goats, sheep and chicken. Bags of grain and spices covered the floor of the car.

I had already begun to imagine my reintroduction to the big city and its life. At every station we stopped, vendors would come running up to the train and crowd around the windows, calling out, "Barbecue chicken! Fish! Bread! Mangoes! Furu-furu!"

After a few hours, the train arrived at the bustling station of Bamako. Hustlers stormed the doors like flies, grabbing people's baggage and carrying it off even before asking permission. These people were looking for work. But Uncle Sumaïla and I hung tightly onto our small bags as we squeezed our way through the noisy crowd. We ducked down to avoid the elbows and shoulders of others moving in all directions.

Finally, after we crossed the entire train station, I said, "It is strange here, Uncle, not like the village. In the village, people know where they are going. But here everyone is running around like a chicken with its head plucked off."

"Yes," replied Uncle Sumaïla. "Everyone comes to the city looking for work, and it is hard to find. What a sad life for many people. This is why I chose the comfort of quiet village life."

It was late morning when we found our way through the noisy crowd of the train station. Outside, we crossed the road to the marketplace where my mother sold spices. But she was not in the market that day, as she had stayed home with a cold.

"Do you know where she lives in Bamako?" Uncle Sumaïla asked a woman named Fifi who had a place next to my mother's empty stand.

"Yes, she lives in a neighborhood called N'golonina near the river."

"How do we get there?" Uncle Sumaïla asked again politely.

"Take this road of Dabanani to where you see many people selling tea and cigarettes. At that place the road

divides in two. Go to your left and continue on until you come to a big electric street lamp. Then continue until the road comes to a dead end. You will now see an old woman named Sira selling spices. She is always present. Sira knows everyone around there and will be able to tell you where Penda lives."

The directions seemed long and complicated, but we reached the dead end and found a tall old woman at the corner selling spices.

As we came closer, Uncle Sumaïla, with his village politeness, knelt down next to the old woman and exchanged greetings.

"Do you by any chance know a lady named Penda?" he asked. "She is my sister-in-law."

"Penda Diakité?"

"*Tigui-tigui*. Exactly. She is the one."

The old woman sent her granddaughter to help us find my mother's house.

When we walked into the courtyard, we could see Mama Penda sitting quietly in the corner by the fire, cooking her evening porridge.

Once she laid eyes upon us, her face lit up and she rose in happiness, raising her hands to the sky as she began to dance and sing a song about the return of her Little Adventurous Bird. She scooped me up into her arms, hugging me tightly.

Then she quickly grabbed Uncle Sumaïla's hand and welcomed both of us. Others in the courtyard joined in to make this happy moment an unexpected celebration.

Later, Mama Penda brought us a warm bucket of water

to bathe in and then fed us green millet porridge with soured milk and a hint of sugar.

Uncle Sumaïla delivered all of the greetings from the village and then announced, "I am here to buy a few things for the preparation of a ceremony that will take place in two days. So I must return to the village tomorrow."

"Don't you want to stay even for a day?" asked Mama Penda.

"People are waiting for me. Besides, I prefer the fresh air of the village."

In the morning, Mama Penda helped Uncle Sumaïla barter in the marketplace. Then we accompanied him to the train station to say goodbye.

From that moment on, I began to learn about the big city and its many troubles. I helped Mama Penda do chores like I did with Grandma. Sometimes I would pound spices and peel and clean vegetables. Other times I carried buckets of water from the public faucets two to three blocks away. I often passed groups of boys my own age seated on the roadside playing cards, drinking tea and shouting at each other.

One day when I was carrying a bucket of cooking water for my mother, one of the boys jumped in my path and asked, "Why are you doing girls' work?"

"I am doing it for my mother," I answered politely.

The boys burst into laughter when they heard my village accent. Then one of them came up to me and gave me a good old punch in my belly while the others shouted, "Welcome to Bamako."

Unable to bear the pain, I threw down the bucket full of

water, grabbed my stomach and ran home. I was so scared that I crawled under Mama Penda's bamboo bed and cried.

But right away, my mother took me by the hand to the boys' parents' house next door and told them of their children's behavior. They were good neighbors and promised Mama Penda to take care of things.

It took time, but in the end, things fell in the right place. The city boys apologized to me and even became my friends.

School

ONE NIGHT Mama asked me to tell some stories to my siblings and my new friends about village life. I began retelling my Grandma stories that night. Even though I did not remember all her magical words, I focused on how I could deliver a message of tolerance through these stories.

Word went around the neighborhood about my stories, and soon children would show up every night to hear them.

I found myself playing the role of an elder storyteller. I also began creating shadow puppets to tell elaborate stories that held morals for the children. I not only made many good friends with the children, but I made friends with their parents, too, who provided a small classroom in the neighborhood for all the activities.

This was the only way some of these children discovered the importance of learning. I told them many stories, taught them to draw the creatures in those stories on hard paper and helped them cut them out for shadow puppet performances at night.

Eventually they became so popular that it was like going to the cinema.

These children were lucky that they discovered the joy of learning through stories and began school at a young age. But for myself, going to school wasn't easy. I had a hard time being accepted in the public school system because of my advanced age. This was a big disappointment for Mama Penda, who had never gone to school herself and wanted her children to know at least how to write their names.

In time, Mama Penda gathered all the documents required and enough money for the transfer to the government school system. Unfortunately, we were rejected by several different schools for no clear reason. The education system was so corrupt that no headmasters had the time to talk to a poor person like Mama Penda, who would not be able to pay the tuition fees plus the bribe money. These heads of schools could recognize who was rich or poor just by looking at them. Only rich families had access to an easy education, even if their children did not take education seriously. This only isolated many poor children, who hung out around street corners with nothing to do and sometimes turned into troublemakers.

So I went back to my old ways of teaching children through storytelling and creating cut-out shadow puppet shows. But Mama Penda never gave up searching for a school for me, and finally she came across an old friend named Jaratu.

Tanti Jaratu accepted me secretly in her fourth grade class despite the fact that I was much older. As the headmaster

often visited the classroom daily, Tanti Jaratu would sometimes push me under a desk covered with a flowery blue
plastic tablecloth and stand in front to mask my legs. But
most of the time she grabbed me under my arm and
dropped me out the window onto the grass below.

Even though Tanti Jaratu was a big and tall woman, and
I was a skinny, bony boy, in time we both got tired of this
exercise. I felt more like a puppet than a student.

As a result of being regularly picked up and dropped out
the window, I acquired a severe chest pain. This prevented
me from going to school for over a month. So Grandma
came to the rescue with a visit to help care for me. This
gave Mama Penda and Tanti Jaratu time to silently negoti-
ate with schools until their determination finally paid off,
and I was accepted in school at the sixth grade level!

Soon after that, Grandma had to leave and go back to
the village. She and Mama Penda held hands, facing each
other.

"Life is never perfect. We can only do our best," said
Mama Penda.

Grandma Sabou chuckled, "Life is a broken story half
lost." Then they both burst into laughing as they
exchanged their final goodbyes.

As I celebrated my new opportunity, I never gave up
teaching with stories, as I realized that learning goes both
ways — to the instructor and to the student.

Bozola

AFTER GRANDMA Sabou went back to the village, Mama Penda, my two brothers, my younger sister and I continued to live in the N'golonina neighborhood near the Djoliba (Niger) River, where Mama Penda had a large vegetable garden. But when a hard time came upon us and we could not afford our daily meals, much less pay the rent, we moved to the Badjalan Trois neighborhood. Mama Penda became the manager of a large compound in exchange for free rent.

However, not only was Badjalan Trois more than six miles away from our old neighborhood N'golonina, but also from the school we children attended.

We struggled for three years, making the long journey back and forth to school on foot, waking early each morning before the sun rose to a cup of hot water for breakfast.

"Have courage, our hardships will end some day," Mama Penda would say.

My older brother and I were responsible for our younger sister Haby, holding her hand through the smog and dense traffic of cars, motorcycles, donkey carts and herds of goats, carrying her on our backs when she was too tired to walk.

We spent all our available time after school caring for our garden, as it was the essential source of our daily meals. We grew a variety of eggplants, cabbages, lettuce, potatoes, beans and onions.

Mama Penda did not like us drawing water from the abrupt edge of the riverbank, fearing someone might get hurt, so we dug a shallow well to water our garden. We had many loyal clients to whom we sold vegetables, so our garden served our financial needs as well as feeding the family.

We eventually moved from Badjalan Trois to the neighborhood of Bozola, where our school was located. We moved in with the family Kane, into which my aunt Kadia had married. This way, my siblings and I would be legally eligible to attend the neighborhood school just a short walk away.

According to my aunt's husband, Sekou, Bozola started out with a single fishing hut. As more and more fishermen settled, it turned into a large fishing village with its own market.

Modern Bozola is now at the very heart of Bamako, the city of millions that grew around it. Bozola has managed to keep alive some of its original village spirit and traditions. A large number of its adobe homes remain undivided even today, and the compounds are interconnected.

The only way to get to some houses was by walking through compound after compound, even during the busiest evening hours when many family members would

be present and exchange formal greetings: "Has the day been peaceful?" and "How is your family's health?" They would then go on to ask about your father, mother, brothers and sisters, until each and every member of your family had been mentioned.

One could literally spend the entire day walking through the old inner alleys of Bozola.

Sadly, the neighborhood could not totally resist urban development, and Bozola became the city's commercial and business district. Soon major streets slashed through parts of the neighborhood. Both sides of the busy streets were lined with merchants' boutiques. The scene was incredibly crowded, with people carrying goods on their heads, on carts, or in old French trucks.

I spent many afternoons as a young man hanging out in front of those shops, reading and writing letters, or doing accounting for those merchants. Many of them came from small towns and had not had the chance to go to school. So I helped them to better their businesses, earning their trust and friendship.

Many of them also came to discover my artistic and storytelling side. During slow business days, I would begin telling simple short stories or jokes with one person. Soon several people would surround me, laughing their heads off. Sometimes they would bring me a page cut out of an old magazine with images they could not understand.

I always gave them my version of what those images meant. At other times I would print their names and paint what they sold on the signboards displayed above their shops. They paid me each time, but I was even prouder that my stories could help these merchant men get through their days.

They came to call me "Amazing Wagué."

✻

In the 1980s, a couple of American artists passed through Bamako on their way to visit the historic city of Timbuktu and met me by accident. I was standing right in front of my courtyard entrance in Bozola. The two were intrigued with a handmade African foosball table and attempted to play a game or two.

The foosball table belonged to my students and me. The money we earned from it was used to buy batteries to project light for our evening puppet shows. However, the Americans were handling the bars in the wrong places, which resulted in grease on their palms.

When they finished their game, I invited them into our compound, giving them soap and water to clean their hands. Afterward, the women convinced them to eat with us. I think they liked it. The next day, they came to thank me with a Michael Jackson music cassette.

This is how the friendship started. They impressed me most when they recognized me as an artist. It was the first time anyone had ever called me that.

I was so excited that I told my mother right away.

Mama responded, "You should be proud. It means that you can work with your hands and heart."

"But everyone works with their hands," I exclaimed.

"Exactly," she said. "Everyone is also an artist."

My American friends continued to visit my compound until they left on their Timbuktu journey. I continued my drawings on cardboard. We would cut out those images with discarded razor blades and use them in our shadow puppet shows.

When my American friends returned from their journey, we connected once again before they went home.

I told them that I appreciated their encouragement, that they had called me an artist.

Heading West

EVEN AFTER the independence of several West African nations from their European colonizers in the late fifties and early sixties, western influences still remained visible in nearly every aspect of life. Though I spent most of my childhood in a small village, no one was entirely immune from the effects of such materialism.

At first a simple radio was considered a high technology that only the wealthiest adults could afford. Bicycles (called iron horses in Bambara) were owned by a handful of rich farmers' sons in our town. They decorated them with vibrant strips of colorful plastic cut from outdoor picnic table covers.

In those days such things allowed one to show off and prove that you were something of a civilized man.

Then the eighties and nineties rolled along, bringing an unlimited inventory of cassette players, radios, Walkmans, Japanese motorcycles and worn-out European cars that attracted the western-educated young men who wanted to prove they were big shots. The cars were nicknamed "Goodbye Europe." They became the biggest polluting machines in the land.

When I first met Ronna, one of the visiting artists who would become my future wife, I was living in Bamako with my mother. I knew just a little bit about the western lifestyle through traveling art exhibitions. I was as busy as a weaver spider, working with all my might doing accounting for the local merchants, painting logos on the fronts of shops, going to school and teaching my "students" in the evenings.

But when I found the courage to pause, meet and get to know Ronna, I realized that there was more to learn about the West than things like jeans and sunglasses, cars and bicycles. It was a whole culture, and she was a tiny window into that culture.

When Ronna invited me to visit her in the United States, I was very excited. But many in my family were worried. Some members had already settled abroad, and their whereabouts were unknown.

One of my uncles said, "Over in the West, one can easily be attached to things. This causes people to focus less on each other." He referred to the old Western cowboy movies in which men fought to their last breath for a piece of shiny gold.

Then, turning his head in my direction, he commented, "Wagué, you should be all right as long as you don't get too distracted by things and get lost in the West. You should see the bright side of it."

Mama Penda quickly jumped in, saying, "Get lost? Not Baba Wagué, my good father's namesake. He will never be greedy enough to get lost anywhere. He will instead continue on the path we set for him, and do the right thing as we expect him to do."

I am sure Mama Penda's confidence had to do with meeting Ronna, who spent a couple of afternoons cooking and chatting by her side. She was impressed by Ronna's courage and had a nice memory of their moments together.

Three months later, my travel date was confirmed. We spent the last few days together as family. Mama Penda told me lots of things about myself as a baby. She said that she was so scared for me, as I was born looking like bones in a bag. My ribs could be counted and my belly was swollen. Both herbal and western doctors could not offer much promise.

Then she patted my head with watery eyes, saying most defiantly, "There is something more powerful than man. You are now a normal human being."

The day I left Bamako, my family accompanied me to the train to Dakar, where I would catch my flight to New York. My clothes were bundled up in one of my mother's scarves.

We were all in tears. They worried about me journeying halfway around the world alone. I worried about how I could make it without them.

In Dakar, Senegal, I was received by my sister Oumou and my cousin Tata Maimouna. They were both happy to see me.

"You're going to America like that?" they exclaimed, looking at my belongings in the small bundle I was holding.

I told them that Mama Penda could not afford a suitcase.

Tata Mai had spent a long time in Europe studying, so she gave me a head's up about how things looked in the

West. My cousin Samba gave me my very first English book with colored pictures. Then they took me to the Sandaga Market to get clothes, shoes and a suitcase.

I was so grateful for their kindness.

Once in New York, my excitement suddenly plummeted. I grew nervous as I faced the reality that the United States was completely different from Mali. Already a one-day journey seemed like a whole month away from Africa.

But after passing through Customs, my eyes lit up when I saw a tall blonde woman leaning against the post at the exit, holding a sign with my name on it.

Not caring who she was, I just ran straight to her and gave her a big hug. Then she introduced herself.

"Je suis Kris, l'amie de Ronna."

I was truly relieved. It was like finding that last missing puzzle piece. I held tight onto her hand the entire time she was arranging for my flight to Portland, Oregon. At that moment, she was the most valuable human on planet Earth.

Kris was friendly and also spoke some French. We entertained each other for several hours before my flight to Portland. Then, at boarding time, I expressed my sincere appreciation and we said goodbye.

Some hours later, I reached Portland and was reunited with Ronna once again.

It was all exciting — to be in my new home, to get to know a new place, to explore new things, and to feel the sweetness of first love.

Soon, after those first few days of meeting and enjoying new friends, people had to return to their daily lives. I began to see the true meaning of the Malian proverb, "Sometimes one can be in the very center of the human crowd, and yet be nostalgic for people." This moment was just like that — missing my family, friends and culture, even as people were weaving all around me.

I began to feel the breeze of loneliness. It was not fun.

In the evenings I went to the community college for English classes. That helped a lot to be around those thinking and seeing a little like me. This experience reminded me of my school and artistic days back in Mali, so I began to write down my memories of my family life in Bambara. Sometimes, when time becomes an issue, I still draw my thoughts, so that later on these drawings will remind me of the right words to write down.

Coming to America has helped me better appreciate my own culture. Drawing and writing about my life makes me feel as if I am present in my culture, speaking my language, joking and laughing with my people. The arts have an unimaginable power to take one on a journey to any part of your past life.

Soon, however, I took a few additional classes at a local art college that resulted in my use of clay to make ceramic pieces. As a well-respected clay artist throughout the United States, Ronna contributed greatly to my courage to stay in America and to my success in becoming a recognized ceramicist.

But the biggest test was yet to come. Ronna — now my wife — asked me to visit her family in Kansas. Ever since we met, she had been telling me about Hoxie, the small town where she grew up in western Kansas.

Speaking just a few words of English, I knew that this would be a test of courage.

With Ronna by my side, her family and I got along just fine. I was assured that they liked me when I passed Ronna's father a handful of cola nuts from Mali as a symbol of respect for an elder, and as proof of my love for his daughter.

This custom was perhaps a little too complicated for Ronna to translate from French to English. Nonetheless, Dr. John and Gloria, my father- and mother-in-law, seemed interested in African cultures. They wanted to know the procedure for a traditional wedding in Mali.

Upon hearing about the thousands of cola nuts and the cow required as dowry for a marriage, and all the intricate steps of showing respect for the elders, my father-in-law smiled and said lightheartedly, "Well, Wagué, you're in luck, then. If you promise to take good care of my daughter, you will be released from owing all those cola nuts and a cow."

We all erupted in a loud burst of laughter.

But what really impressed me was meeting Ronna's grandfather, also named John. He was ninety-six and extremely smart. He spoke German, French and, of course, English.

After a happy, soft hug with Ronna, he motioned his head toward me and said, "Is this the mister?" He shook my hand and motioned to us to sit on the sofa facing him. I did not find him too chatty but I knew that the wise man's head was full of knowledge. I was lucky to know him until he was ninety-nine.

Over the years, I have come to recognize my in-laws' kindness and generosity more and more, and how lucky I have been to become part of such a family. Every July, we visit with family and friends in Hoxie and enjoy the county fair.

After my second visit, I started to realize there are many similarities with my village Kassaro in the southwestern part of Mali. People in both places politely take time for greetings as though they mean it. The stormy wild weather is typically the most talked-about subject. People carefully scan the sky and watch the movements of the clouds to prepare for thunderstorms and tornadoes.

In the late evening at the county fair, one can feel the presence of almost the whole town. It takes me back to the old days in Kassaro, where summer festivities took place in the town square. As in Hoxie, each and every able body had to help out to make the festival a success. Even my brother-in-law Karl, the only dentist in town, and his wife, Lu, sell drinks at the fair to help their small town.

I have always believed that the solution to all of our problems lies within ourselves. It is like that American saying, "What goes around, comes around."

If you help to raise up the town you live in, you will rise along with it.

A Final Memory

WHEN I LEFT for America, I was worried about Grandma Sabou, as she was a few months past one hundred rainy seasons. Two years later, I took Ronna back to Mali to introduce her to Grandma Sabou. She was extremely proud of both of us and held our hands together for a long moment while we were seated next to her.

Ronna spent much of her time in Mali with my sisters and other women in the neighborhood — shopping, braiding hair or cooking. But she could not understand why, after the formal greeting, my sisters-in-law would ask, "Did you sleep well? Did your husband treat you right last night?"

"Yes," she would answer. But the women would ask these questions in a whisper, and whenever she tried to get me to translate, they would quickly wave their hands, "Never mind."

Finally I explained to her that African women recognize that all women share common problems and must boost each other's morale. Unlike in America, African women and men form separate groups — even during social events — to share this bond.

But one evening, my sister-in-law Jelika sent for me to clear up a misunderstanding. I was surprised, as they never wanted men to know what they shared as women.

"Wagué, your wife must love you way too much. If I understand her, I think she said that a man and a woman should be equal."

"She is right," I responded.

"Of course you will want that, since you're a man," they shouted.

"Ronna!" Jelika and Jeneba called loudly. "You do not want to be equal to a man. No woman in the world wants that. You know why? Because men have always wanted to be equal to us, the women."

"Yes," shouted others standing behind, with big laughs. "We're always outsmarting them. This is why we are proud to be women — the mothers of kings and cripples, the mothers of rich and poor. We are women!"

Although none of those women had gone to school or had traveled around the world, it did not matter. Ronna confirmed that she partially agreed with my sister-in-law's point of view. They went back to their chanting and dancing as I walked back to my metal chair under the mango tree.

"Wagué, I really like my African sisters. I like the fact that everything is discussed in the open and solved in the open," Ronna said later.

In spite of being from a small Kansas town, Ronna had found ways to blend firmly with my African families and friends.

Just as Ronna was worried that I would be too lonely in America, I was worried about how she would handle the never-ending jokes in my culture. But Mama Penda has always said, "Take things one day at a time and do not worry too much about tomorrow, because perhaps there is nothing in tomorrow to worry about."

✳

IT HAS BEEN more than two decades since that first visit back home. Grandma died at one hundred and four rainy seasons, but we have never forgotten her. I am so pleased that she got to meet Ronna and welcome her into our family.

Grandma Sabou will always be in the center of our family heart. Mama Penda is now over eighty rainy seasons and enjoying her own grandchildren and the care provided by her children. She has become the true example of her own proverb that says, "A child is like a tree. If you take good care of it, you will enjoy its shade later."

As an adult now, with my own family to care for, I have come to clearly see the unbelievable effort others have made for me. Many people were involved in raising little me in the village, and they endowed me with gifts I will carry my entire life. They gave me the knowledge from their own life experiences and handed me stories they heard from their elders.

These are the true treasures that I will cherish forever.